WILLIAM O'BR

BRONZE AGE COPPER MINING IN BRITAIN AND IRELAND

THE
PAUL HAMLYN
LIBRARY

———•———

DONATED BY
THE PAUL HAMLYN
FOUNDATION
TO THE
BRITISH MUSEUM

———•———

Opened December 2000

SHIRE ARCHAEOLOGY

2

622 343 094 / OBR

THE
BRITISH
MUSEUM
THE PAUL HAMLYN LIBRARY

Cover photograph
Fire-setting in a bronze age mine.
(Photograph: William O'Brien.)

British Library Cataloguing in Publication Data
O'Brien, William, 1961-
Bronze age copper mining in Britain and Ireland. - (Shire archaeology; 71)
1. Copper mines and mining - Great Britain - History
2. Copper mines and mining - Ireland - History
3. Bronze age - Great Britain
4. Bronze age - Ireland
I. Title
622.3'43'0941
ISBN 0747803218

Published by
SHIRE PUBLICATIONS LTD
Cromwell House, Church Street, Princes Risborough,
Buckinghamshire HP27 9AA, UK.

Series Editor: James Dyer.

Copyright © William O'Brien 1996.
William O'Brien is hereby identified as the author of this work in
accordance with section 77 of the Copyright, Designs and Patents Act 1988.

All rights reserved.
No part of this publication may be reproduced or transmitted
in any form or by any means, electronic or mechanical,
including photocopy, recording, or any information storage
and retrieval system, without permission in writing
from the publishers.

ISBN 0 7478 0321 8.

First published 1996.

Printed in Great Britain by
CIT Printing Services, Press Buildings,
Merlins Bridge, Haverfordwest, Dyfed SA61 1XF.

Contents

Acknowledgements

I wish to thank my wife Madeline, colleagues Angela Gallagher and John Waddell, and University College, Galway, for assistance with the preparation of this book. The Irish content is based largely on the author's own research, in collaboration with many specialists and archaeological assistants. The British evidence is mainly drawn from the work of the Great Orme research team and the Early Mines Research Group. I would particularly like to thank Brenda Craddock, Paul Craddock, Andrew Dutton, David Gale, Robert Ixer, Tony Lewis, John Pickin and Simon Timberlake for the use of published material.

List of illustrations

1
Introduction

During the bronze age period of prehistory there was widespread adoption of copper-alloy metallurgy across Europe. The knowledge of metallurgy, first appearing in the Near East, developed in stone age Europe as early as 4500 BC. Through technical advances, most parts of Europe adopted copper-tin alloys, or 'bronze', by 2000 BC, and this led soon afterwards to fully metal-using societies. In technological terms, the bronze age in Britain and Ireland is generally taken to span the period from the earliest introduction of metal, around 2500 BC, to the slow transition to iron metallurgy after 600 BC.

Metal made an important contribution to almost every aspect of bronze age life, from art to warfare and advances in agriculture, woodworking and related crafts. The new technology opened up a range of new fabrication possibilities, which bronze age craft workers were quick to exploit. The supply of metal to regions lacking local sources laid the basis for an enduring trade network in a range of commodities. The exploitation of the new resource and this new dependency between different regions obviously had profound social implications. Individuals and groups may have emerged to control production and distribution for their own benefit. In this way metal contributed in no small measure to the rise of social hierarchies across bronze age Europe.

The bronze age in Europe is marked by a great volume of metal, consisting of many thousands of copper, bronze and gold objects. The success of bronze metallurgy is partly linked to the wide availability of copper ores. Prehistoric copper mines have been found in many countries, most notably the Balkans, Austria and Spain. Britain and Ireland, long regarded as prolific centres of bronze age metallurgy, were also major sources of copper. This short account outlines the evidence for bronze age copper mining in these islands, its technology and the many important discoveries in this field in recent times.

2
Distribution

The distribution of bronze age copper mines today clearly reflects the spread of metalliferous ore bodies across Britain and Ireland. This is not to say that all ore deposits were available for mining in the bronze age. Many locations worked for copper in recent centuries would not have been accessible to the prehistoric miner in terms of technology. Conversely, many locations where copper was mined in the bronze age were not economically viable for mining in recent centuries, with Mount Gabriel in west Cork the most extreme example of this. Accessibility was vital to the bronze age miners, whose dedicated search for copper led them to explore even the poorest of ore sources. The explanation for this clearly lies in the perceived value of copper, which maintained its status as a valuable commodity throughout the bronze age.

The evidence

The recognition of bronze age copper mines today depends chiefly on the discovery of stone mining hammers in association with primitive mine workings. The latter are usually marked by the use of fire to shatter rock, which could then be removed by pounding with the stone hammers. The mines resulting from this process have smooth concave walls on which the diffuse marks of hammer battering are sometimes visible. These workings can take several forms, depending on the geological setting and scale of operations. However, they are nearly always associated with dumps of broken rock spoil rich in charcoal and stone hammers. Other activity areas around these mines would have included hut shelters, cooking hearths, equipment and fuel stores and, most probably, locations where copper ore was smelted to metal. Particularly vulnerable to destruction by later mining, these ancillary areas are usually not visible today, often masked by rock spoil or blanket-bog growth in mountain areas.

The known distribution of bronze age copper mines in Britain and Ireland focuses chiefly on two metalliferous regions: mid and north Wales and the Cork-Kerry area (figure 1). A survey has identified as many as twenty-six locations in Wales where ancient stone hammers were found during mining in recent centuries. Four of these sites have been radiocarbon-dated to the bronze age and it is likely that many others also date to this period. The best-known of these early copper mines is located on the Great Orme, a limestone headland near Llandudno on the North Wales coast. This is the site of what may well have been

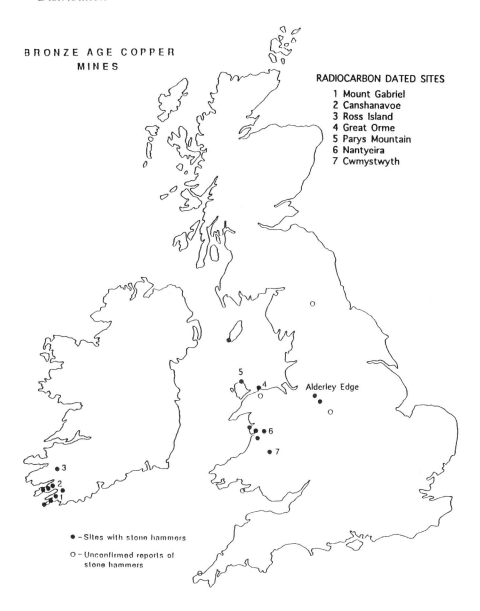

BRONZE AGE COPPER
MINES

RADIOCARBON DATED SITES
1 Mount Gabriel
2 Canshanavoe
3 Ross Island
4 Great Orme
5 Parys Mountain
6 Nantyeira
7 Cwmystwyth

Alderley Edge

● – Sites with stone hammers

○ – Unconfirmed reports of
stone hammers

1. Distribution of bronze age copper mines in Britain and Ireland.

the largest copper mine in bronze age Britain, worked over a thousand-year period (figure 2). On the island of Anglesey, radiocarbon dating has confirmed bronze age mining at the well-known site of Parys Mountain, which was one of the largest copper mines in Europe in the eighteenth and nineteenth centuries.

In mid Wales there is an important group of primitive copper mines in the mountains east of Aberystwyth. These include the well-known copper

2. Surface trench workings of bronze age date located around a nineteenth-century shaft at the Great Orme copper mine, North Wales.

mine high in the mountains at Cwmystwyth. This has now been dated to the bronze age, as has the site of Nantyreira on the eastern slopes of Plynlimon close to another primitive copper mine at Nantyrickets. Other early copper mines marked by the use of stone hammers have been identified on either side of the Dyfi estuary and in the area north of the river Rheidol. Unpublished radiocarbon dates for two sites located south of the Dyfi estuary, namely Borth bog and Llancynfelin, appear to confirm bronze age copper mining in this area. In South Wales, stone hammers linked to primitive copper mining have been found at Llandovery and on the Gower peninsula near Swansea.

Outside Wales there are remarkably few finds of early copper workings or stone hammers from famous ore fields like the Peak District or Cornwall. The best-known ancient copper mine in England is at Alderley Edge in Cheshire. Nineteenth-century antiquarian digging and recent survey strongly point to bronze age activity at this and the nearby Mottram St Andrew mine. Stone mining hammers have also been found at Ecton in Staffordshire, pointing to possible bronze age copper mining in the Peak District. There is very little evidence of early copper mining known at present from northern Britain, though stone hammers have been reported at Bradda Head on the Isle of Man. The absence of bronze age mines in Scotland would appear anomalous, given the well-known concentration of bronze age monuments in many metalliferous areas.

A continuing problem is the lack of evidence for bronze age copper mining in south-west England. The copper and tin lodes of Cornwall and Devon have a long history of mining, stretching back to Roman and medieval times. The nineteenth-century copper-mining industry in this region was one of the biggest producers in Europe. While there are growing indications of alluvial tin extraction in Cornwall in bronze age times, no evidence for copper mining in this period has yet been identified. This partly reflects a lack of archaeological excavation and interference from later industrial mining, though documentary sources from the nineteenth-century industry are surprisingly silent on primitive copper mine discoveries. The destruction caused by industrial mining and the difficulty of dating primitive technology used into medieval times have made this a difficult, though challenging, area for the fieldworker. Most researchers confidently predict that bronze age copper mines will some day be identified in Cornwall.

In Ireland there are several reports of 'old men's workings' in the nineteenth-century mining literature from the Wicklow, Tipperary and Waterford ore fields, but the precise status of these finds remains unknown. The focus of interest, in terms of bronze age copper mining, continues to be the Cork-Kerry region, where several important discoveries were made in the nineteenth century. A number of these have been the subject of detailed investigation in recent times. The best-known group is the Mount Gabriel-type workings, small surface mines located on sedimentary copper beds in the Old Red Sandstone and worked with fire-setting and stone hammers.

The largest concentration of these mines is located on Mount Gabriel in the Mizen peninsula of west Cork, where over thirty workings, dating to between 1700 and 1500 BC, have been identified in an unspoiled blanket-bog environment. Elsewhere in this peninsula Mount Gabriel-type workings have been identified at Boulysallagh, Callaros Oughter, Carrigacat, Ballyrisode and probably Toormore. Similar workings may also be present at a large primitive copper mine discovered in the mid nineteenth century at Derrycarhoon in this area. Mount Gabriel-type mines have also been identified at three sites in the Beara peninsula in west Cork, namely Crumpane, Tooreen and Canshanavoe; the last site is also radiocarbon-dated to the bronze age.

Although no Mount Gabriel-type mines have been found in County Kerry, primitive mine workings are known from the western end of the Iveragh peninsula. They include the rather curious site of St Crohane's Cave on Coad Mountain where a fire-set cave on the back of a quartz lode was apparently reused as a monk's hermitage in early Christian times. The focus of bronze age copper mining in Kerry rests firmly on the Killarney lakes area, where a major site has been discovered at Ross Island. Ongoing research here has identified an early phase of copper mining dating to 2400-2000 BC.

The known distribution of bronze age copper mines today is undoubtedly biased in several ways. Many important sites have almost certainly been destroyed or their surface visibility masked by mining in more recent times. Documentary sources on the discovery of early workings in later mining are mostly limited to the nineteenth century, and even then the reporting of finds was very inconsistent. Natural erosion may explain why there are practically no known bronze age copper mines on the many coastal cliff exposures of copper mineralisation around Britain and Ireland. The visibility of inland sites is affected by blanket-bog growth over the past three thousand years and by forestry in recent times, while the location of many mines in difficult upland terrain does not help in their discovery.

The distribution may also reflect investigation patterns in recent times, as research has tended to follow those discoveries documented in historic mining. This is particularly true of those sites linked to the use of fire-setting and stone hammers, which recent radiocarbon evidence would suggest are almost exclusively bronze age. While new discoveries remain to be made in other parts of Britain and Ireland, it remains to be seen whether this fieldwork will significantly change our focus on mid and north Wales and south-west Ireland. Present research is clearly biased towards the discovery of mines at a very primitive level of technology, which may well have been superseded in many regions as the bronze age progressed.

The search for copper

Copper-bearing rocks or ores are often very complex in their geological setting, mineralogy and chemistry. While modern mining is more concerned with tonnage, bronze age miners targeted easily accessible deposits of surface ore (figure 3). Obviously the copper minerals had to be present in a sufficient concentration to allow them to be extracted and smelted. Several mineral occurrences do not satisfy this requirement and should

3. Coastal exposure of sedimentary copper beds, west Cork.

not be used in any resource analysis of early metallurgy. There are no secondary sources of copper, comparable to the alluvial stream deposits of gold and tin used in the bronze age, which could have contributed significantly to the supply of metal in this period. Mineralised boulders are occasionally found dispersed in the glacial drift, but for a concentrated ore source it was necessary to mine a bedrock deposit.

Ore deposits in the glaciated landscapes of Britain and Ireland are not generally marked by outcrops of leached iron oxide or 'gossans', which are a feature of many ore bodies in southern Europe. While many mineralised exposures were scraped clean by the ice-sheets, others were covered by a thick mantle of drift and have been found only with the aid of geochemistry and other modern exploration techniques. The 'science' of ore prospecting in the bronze age was far simpler, based on a careful inspection of rock outcrop in areas of favourable geology and an empirical understanding of mineral colours and densities. This is borne out by the distribution of bronze age mines today, which are generally found in areas of high rock exposure, typically in inland mountain settings. A long history of stone age settlement in these areas, which included a search for suitable hard rocks to make tools, led in time to the discovery of mineralised outcrops streaked with the bright colours of secondary copper minerals like malachite and azurite. While possibly first appreciated as a source of pigment, the significance of these discoveries became apparent with the rapid spread of metallurgy across Britain and Ireland after 2500 BC.

4. Primitive copper mine, Tooreen, west Cork.

3
History of research

Since the mid 1980s many exciting discoveries have been made relating to bronze age copper mining in Britain and Ireland. It is surprising that this field of research was so neglected until recent years, given the long interest in mining history, particularly in Britain. This is partly explained by the strong historical focus which these studies traditionally have had in an area dominated by geologists, mining historians and industrial archaeologists. Many scholars, limited by their documentary sources to activity of Roman and later date, have been slow to recognise the great antiquity of copper mining. Prehistorians, for their part, have been reluctant to explore an area where considerable geological expertise was required to investigate often complex mining sites. Moreover, a general pessimism prevailed as to the ability of ancient metal mines to survive the large-scale industrial mining of recent centuries.

Research since the 1960s into early copper mining in the Middle East, the Balkans, Austria and Spain has helped raise the profile of this subject.

These studies emphasise the potential of even the most intensively reworked ore deposits to produce some archaeological record of early mining. Also relevant here is the progress made by various scientific programmes set up since the 1950s to analyse early copper and bronze metalwork in Europe. The limited success of this research in terms of identifying metal sources, at a time when studies of stone axe petrology were making great advances, brought our poor understanding of bronze age copper mining sharply into focus. While this emerged as a major research priority, it was still left to a small group of fieldworkers to make the many significant advances in this field since the mid 1980s (figure 4).

Britain

The great expansion in British mining in the eighteenth and nineteenth centuries led to the discovery of primitive workings in many metalliferous districts. This was a time of great loss to the archaeological record, when many 'old men's workings', attributed to the Romans or to shadowy Phoenicians, were destroyed. Yet as early as 1744 Lewis Morris, antiquarian and Crown Agent, speculated that the stone hammers found in many copper mines in mid Wales were used before there was knowledge of iron. Unfortunately it was almost two centuries before this prescient observation could be realised in archaeological terms.

The investigations at Alderley Edge by Professor Boyd Dawkins in 1874, and subsequently in the early 1900s by the antiquarians Roeder and Graves, stand out for particular attention. They argued strongly that the earliest phase of mining at this site was bronze age and that the use of fire-setting and stone hammer extraction was clearly separate from Roman and later mining. While lacking hard scientific evidence to support this conclusion, their work opened up the possibility of very early copper mining at a time when many of the Alderley Edge remains were being destroyed.

The next major move was made in 1935, when the British Association for the Advancement of Science established a committee to investigate early metal mining in Wales. The secretary was Oliver Davies, a leading authority on Roman mining in Europe. As part of his survey programme in mid and north Wales, Davies trenched a number of spoil tips containing stone hammers at Parys Mountain, the Great Orme, Cwmystwyth and Nantyreira. With no datable artefacts and without the advantage of radiocarbon dating, Davies concluded that the stone hammer phase at these sites was of the Roman or 'Old Celtic' period. While his basic conclusions are wrong, this work did draw attention to four important sites which fifty years later would be linked conclusively to bronze age copper mining.

Growing interest in early metal sources in Britain eventually led to a great surge of interest in the 1980s. Work began with the underground explorations at the Great Orme of an interested amateur, Duncan James, as early as 1976. James succeeded in radiocarbon-dating charcoal from fire-setting firmly associated with stone hammers and bone tools in these early workings. The date of 2940+80 BP (HAR-4845), calibrated to 1395-935 BC, provided the first scientific evidence of bronze age copper mining in Britain. James's work on the Orme was followed by surveys carried out by Andy Lewis and the Great Orme Exploration Society in the late 1980s, with extensive surface excavations carried out by Andrew Dutton for Gwynedd Archaeological Trust in 1989.

Between 1985 and 1987 a group of interested geologists and mining historians, led by Simon Timberlake, formed the Early Mines Research Group to investigate early copper mining in Wales. Radiocarbon dates from trial excavations at Parys Mountain, Cwmystwyth and Nantyreira provided conclusive evidence of early to middle bronze age copper mining in this part of Britain. Research in recent years has focused on a more detailed investigation of the Cwmystwyth site, while a search of the mining literature has identified many more copper mines in Wales marked by a primitive phase of fire-setting and stone hammers. This pioneering phase of research in Wales came to fruition with the publication of a major conference on bronze age copper mining, held in Snowdonia National Park in November 1989.

Ireland

Nineteenth-century metal mining in Ireland was an offshoot of a larger British industry and its progress also led to the discovery of many primitive mine workings. These finds excited some antiquarian interest at a time when the excellence of early Irish metalwork was beginning to be appreciated. Most attention focused on the Cork-Kerry region, where several early copper mines had been discovered. With little medieval (and obviously no Roman) mining to complicate matters, there is a clear contrast here between workings of the nineteenth-century industry and the primitive technology found in sites recently dated to the bronze age.

The first of these early mine discoveries resulted from an attempt to work a copper mine on the shores of Ross Island in Killarney in the eighteenth and early nineteenth centuries. The discovery of primitive mines worked with fire and stone hammers attracted much attention from antiquarians and visitors. These ancient workings were attributed by many to the Danish incursions into Ireland. However, Sir Richard Griffith's speech to the Royal Dublin Society in 1828 demonstrates that this connection was already being viewed with scepticism. Scholars began to delve into the prehistoric past to try to explain these finds. This speculation increased with the publication in 1861 of Sir William Wilde's catalogue of copper and bronze antiquities, which drew attention to the technical achievements

5. Mount Gabriel-type mines discovered at Boulysallagh, west Cork, during nineteenth-century mineral prospecting.

of what would soon be known as the bronze age period in Ireland. The West Carbery mining district of west Cork was the setting for many important primitive mine discoveries in the nineteenth-century mining period. These included the discovery in 1846 of fire-setting evidence and stone tools in early workings at Derrycarhoon, while stone hammers were found under 2 metres of peat in a mine at Boulysallagh in the early 1850s (figure 5). The thickness of peat growth at both sites impressed many commentators as to the antiquity of this mining. This was reinforced in 1854 when a cache of twelve polished stone axes was found inside a small copper working at Ballyrisode, also in the Mizen peninsula (figure 6). Nevertheless, most scholars continued to urge caution on the dating of these primitive copper mines right up the 1950s.

Most attention on bronze age copper mining in Ireland has hitherto focused on the discovery of over thirty small workings along the slopes of Mount Gabriel in the Mizen peninsula. This site came to prominence in

6. Mount Gabriel-type working at Ballyrisode, west Cork, where a cache of polished stone axes was found in 1854. The photograph shows the antiquarian trench dug in the course of this discovery.

1929 when the geologist Tom Duffy concluded that these inclined openings in the Old Red Sandstone must be prehistoric.This was confirmed in 1966 when another geologist, John Jackson, submitted a charcoal sample from a trench across one of these early spoil dumps to the Vienna Radium Institute. The resulting date of 3450+120 BP (VRI-66), calibrated to 2135-1510 BC,

7. Peat accumulation infilling a bronze age mine on Mount Gabriel. This peat formed as a result of grasses and other vegetation blowing into the open flooded working.

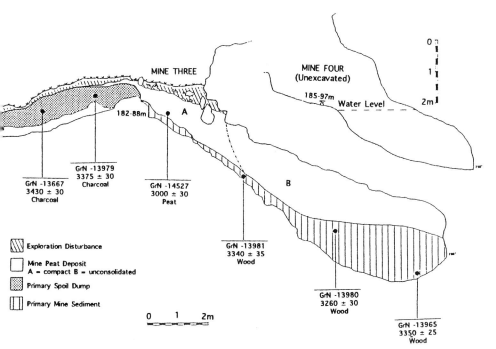

8. Mine 3 infill sequence and radiocarbon dates, Mount Gabriel.

provided the first independent scientific evidence of bronze age copper mining in Ireland or Britain.

In 1982 the present author began a programme of survey and excavation on the Mount Gabriel mines as part of a doctoral study. This work culminated in 1985 with a large-scale investigation of one of these bronze age mine camps (figure 7). The Mount Gabriel study was followed by an investigation of other early copper mines in south-west Ireland, most notably the continuing research at Ross Island, Killarney. Radiocarbon dates and the discovery of early Beaker pottery have confirmed this site as the oldest copper mine presently known in north-western Europe.

The impact of radiocarbon dating

Research into bronze age copper mining has been dogged by speculation and controversy about the dating of these sites, with at least one commentator continuing to doubt their very existence! Much of this debate centred on the very real problem of dating holes in the ground which cannot be connected to datable artefacts, such as pottery. Radiocarbon dating has made an enormous contribution, from 1966, when the very first date was obtained on Mount Gabriel, to the time of writing, when there are almost fifty determinations from at least eight sites in Britain and Ireland (figures 8 and 40). The application of this dating method has been helped by the practice of fire-setting in these early mines, which left considerable fuel residues in the form of charcoal and waterlogged wood with tooling marks. Radiocarbon dating of what is mostly young roundwood fuel has placed this mining firmly in the bronze age, as do the many dates for animal bone from these sites. The stone axes from Ballyrisode and the discovery of early Beaker pottery and worked flint at Ross Island are a further confirmation of this prehistoric date.

Radiocarbon dates for these British and Irish copper mines fall largely within the early and middle bronze age, *c*.1800-1300 BC. Ross Island appears to belong to an earlier phase of mining in the final neolithic/copper-using period, *c*.2400-2000 BC, while the Great Orme extraction may have continued into later bronze age times, ending shortly after 1000 BC. The clarity of this evidence is remarkable when one considers the quandary in which early scholars found themselves over dating. To paraphrase the nineteenth-century Cork antiquarian John Windele, radiocarbon dating has allowed us to 'verify those much disputed statements of the early working of mines in Ireland, which some would have treated as figments'.

4
Technology

The ability to mine metal ore from the earth's surface has its origins in many thousands of years of rock extraction in the stone age. The basic techniques of bronze age copper mining find parallels in the hard rock quarries and flint mines of the neolithic. The primitive technology applied to this early copper mining contrasts with the complex processes of the metal workshop. Indeed, metal tools are not used in the earliest copper mining efforts, apart from bronze axes and blades used to collect and process wood.

The approach to mining

The approach to early copper mining was determined to a large degree by the geological setting and surface exposure of the ore body. Bronze age mines are always located on mineralised exposures, with efforts usually focused on the 0-10 metre surface zone where copper mineralisation was often enriched by percolating water. Once deposits had been discovered at surface, bronze age miners were able to follow the brightly coloured copper minerals underground, often to surprising depths. In doing so they displayed a knowledge of the geological environment gained only by long hours at the mine face.

We can distinguish here between mining carried out on sources of concentrated mineralisation, such as quartz-sulphide veins, and those situations where the ore is dispersed through a particular rock stratum. In all cases, the miners came quickly to understand various geological controls on the mineralisation, whether it be the dolomitisation process at Great Orme or the copper beds of a certain colour and lithology on Mount Gabriel. In metallurgical terms they also learned how to adapt to different types of copper mineral within an ore body. Limited by the visibility of their mineral target and focusing where possible on rich, highly accessible mineralisation, these miners displayed a surprising ability to work copper showings which would not have been viable in nineteenth-century mining.

Rock extraction

Bronze age mines are usually surface workings in the form of opencasts and surface pits, narrow trench cuttings and inclined drift openings on scarped exposures. True underground mining is also known, most notably on the Great Orme, where a complex system of tunnels and rock caverns has been explored to a depth of 70 metres. In pursuing

9. Mine 3, Mount Gabriel, after excavation. Note the influence of folding on the shape of the mine entrance.

these workings the miners had to adapt to the structure of the surrounding rock. Mineralised strata and lodes are often found in a contorted state where the host rock has been folded or fractured through faulting. The influence of fold structure is well illustrated in the accompanying photograph of Mine 3 on Mount Gabriel (figure 9). Yet even here, working in hard siliceous rocks, the miners were starting to make that transition from strata-bound extraction to tunnelling at will across the geological structure.

The size of these bronze age workings was dictated by the geological setting, the available technology and, obviously, by the perceived richness of the mineralisation. The success of individual mining efforts may be measured on Mount Gabriel, where a spread of over thirty workings from less than 1 metre up to 12 metres in inclined depth reflects the relative concentration of copper minerals at different outcrops. While much bronze age mining took this form of 'flitting' from one mineralised exposure to the next, the large workings discovered at Ross Island, Cwmystwyth and the Great Orme all reflect a concentration of mining effort on particularly rich deposits over a long time (up to a thousand years in the case of the Orme!).

Bronze age copper mines are usually marked by an economy of effort, where only those rock types that actually contained ore minerals were extracted. Mine development in the modern sense was largely unknown, though clearly we should not underestimate the skill and organisation required in this early search for metal. While a large underground mine like the Great Orme may never have been planned out in the modern sense, the miners clearly had a strategy adapted to their level of technology, which in time led to the large complex of workings we see today.

Various factors limited the size of these bronze age mines, from geological controls to operational difficulties posed by roof collapse, water seepage, ventilation and lighting. External factors may have included ritual beliefs and superstition and a fluctuating demand or 'need' for metal as the bronze age progressed in different regions. When comparing the size of individual operations, we must distinguish between the mining of hard siliceous rocks and the extraction of softer geologies, of which the dolomitised limestone on the Great Orme is an extreme example. Bronze age miners worked in many different geological environments, where hardness depended not just on rock type but on the degree of surface weathering and the influence of microstructures like cleavage.

10. Reconstruction of a fire-setting operation in an early copper mine. (Drawing: Conor Duggan.)

11. Oak roundwood with axe tooling marks used as fuel in Mine 3, Mount Gabriel.

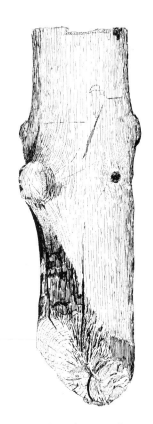

To extract hard rock, bronze age copper miners across Ireland and Britain resorted to a remarkably similar range of techniques, most notably the use of fire in combination with stone hammers, as well as wooden and bone tools. Fire-setting is a rock extraction method of great antiquity, found in primitive mining contexts the world over; it was successfully applied to copper mining in parts of Europe even up to the nineteenth century. Its basic application involves burning wood fires against the mine face, causing it to weaken (figure 10). In some cases the heat-fracturing effect may be increased by sudden water quenching. Rock can then be removed from the shattered face by pounding it with stone hammers, used hafted or hand-held. The efficiency of this fire-setting technique depends very much on the rock type.

Fire-setting in these mines consumed a large amount of wood, mostly gathered from deciduous woodland in the immediate vicinity. Operations on Mount Gabriel consumed many thousands of tonnes of roundwood fuel, which clearly had implications for the surrounding environment. Tree-ring studies on an assemblage of wood, mostly oak and hazel, found in a waterlogged mine on this mountain point to some form of organised fuel collection. More recently it has been possible to study the impact of wood collection on local tree growth through pollen studies developed by Tim Mighall in the University of Coventry. Tooling marks point to the use of bronze axes and blades in gathering this Mount Gabriel fuel (figure 11), while the use of polished stone axes in tree felling is suggested by the Ballyrisode find of 1854.

In removing rock the bronze age miners exploited any fracture weakness such as cleavage or joint planes, using pick-like implements and fingers to prise out the heat-shattered fragments. Pointed wooden sticks and picks, carefully carved from hazel stems, used for this purpose have been discovered on Mount Gabriel (figure 12). Bone fragments found in spoil tips at Ross Island, Cwmystwyth and the Great Orme may point to the use of antler picks in a manner reminiscent of neolithic flint mines. No metal mining tools of bronze age date are known from any of these insular copper mines, though bronze fragments have been discovered at the Great Orme. Metal picks and mining tools do not appear to have been used in earlier bronze age mining, though some antiquarian discoveries hint at their introduction towards the end of this period, when they may even have replaced stone hammers.

12. Reconstruction of underground mining, Mount Gabriel. (Drawing: Conor Duggan.)

The Great Orme stands apart from other bronze age copper mines in the soft nature of its ore-bearing geology, which partly explains the scale of working visible today. The use of fire-setting and stone hammers in this site appears to have been restricted to encounters with hard rock. Instead, the miners were able to use pointed animal bones as picks and

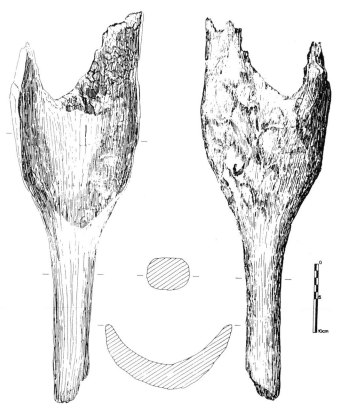

13. Alder shovel found in Mine 3, Mount Gabriel.

gouges to extract copper minerals from the rotten dolomite and shales around the ore channels. These simple bone points have left their mark on the mine walls, which also show traces of pounding with stone hammers.

Broken rock extract and charcoal residues from these bronze age mines were generally removed to the surface for sorting, using shovels and containers of some kind. In the case of deeper mines like the Orme, there is evidence of underground sorting and the stacking of 'deads', or waste rock, in abandoned tunnels in a very organised fashion. The use of wooden shovels has been confirmed on Mount Gabriel, where a short-handled example, carved from a single piece of alder, and fragments of several others were discovered in 1987 (figure 13). More recently, a wooden shovel found in nineteenth-century diggings in the Alderley Edge mine has been radiocarbon-dated to the early bronze age. From Ross Island comes evidence for the use of cattle shoulder-blade bones as scoops or shovels in early copper mines, an implement type again paralleled in neolithic flint mining. While no containers have been identified in these bronze age mines, baskets or sacks would have been necessary to transport finely broken rock around the site.

While many bronze age copper mines were surface operations, some provision for underground access had to be made in the case of deeper workings. Foot notches were cut in the floor of the steeply inclined Mount Gabriel workings and wooden step planks were also used to

14. Interior of Mine 3, Mount Gabriel.

allow access (figure 14). Vertical workings required ropes and possibly ladders made from tied saplings, but so far no cordage has been found in these Irish-British mines. The discovery of a notched tree-trunk in the Derrycarhoon site in 1846 may point to the use of this type of primitive ladder, though this particular find has not been dated.

Some provision also had to be made for ventilation and lighting in deeper mines. The underground workings in the Great Orme had numerous connections to the surface for this purpose and there is some evidence for deliberate 'deads stacking' to control air-flow for fires lit at depths of at least 30 metres. Fire-setting at this depth may have been accompanied by great discomfort, particularly at the time when the fires had to be lit . In many bronze age mines fire-setting took place as part of a daily work routine, whereby miners vacated the underground workings to concentrate ore at the surface, collect service materials like wood, prepare mine equipment or simply rest and cook food.

Miners may have used animal oil or fat lamps to light their work underground but no examples have been found. The discovery of several hundred partly charred splints of pine in one waterlogged mine on

Mount Gabriel points to another source of underground illumination (figure 15). Pine is a resinous wood which burns with a bright smoky flame. Pine splints similar to the Mount Gabriel examples are known from early copper mines in Austria and Spain, where also they appear

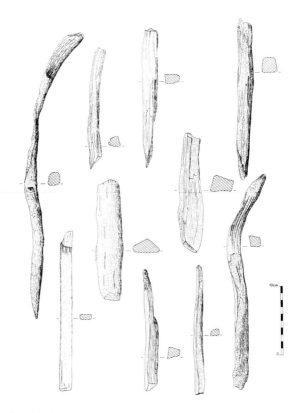

15. Pine splints found inside Mine 3, Mount Gabriel.

to have been used as torches.

Ancient copper miners, like their modern counterparts, had much to fear from roof collapse and flooding. However, there are few instances of roof collapse in any of these bronze age mines, partly because the mining process did not disturb the underground rock strata in the way modern explosives do. In addition, fire-setting tends to create workings with smooth load-bearing walls, which probably explains why evidence for support timbering has never been found in these bronze age mines. Neither is there any indication of mine fatalities, as none of the Irish-

British sites have yet produced human remains or mortuary evidence . There can be little doubt that accidents, comparable to the fate which befell the 'Copper Man' from Chuquicamata in northern Chile (who was trapped down an early copper mine), were also commonplace in bronze age workings in Europe.

Flooding was undoubtedly a worry in any mine operation depending on underground fire-setting. With the exception of the Great Orme, most bronze age workings are permanently flooded today. This may have been less of a problem in earlier bronze age times, when the insular climate was marked by lower rainfall levels, as reflected in the more restricted spread of upland blanket bog at that time. This may have changed in the later bronze age after 1200 BC, when a marked climatic deterioration may have had consequences for many long-term bronze age mines. To limit water seepage into open workings, the miners may have confined their operations to the summer months, though the seasonality of bronze age copper mining is poorly understood. Once operations began at sites like Mount Gabriel, work probably continued twenty-four hours a day to minimise the likelihood of flooding, with hand-bailing using animal skins or some such container carried out in some instances. The only evidence for drainage equipment comes from Cwmystwyth, where excavations uncovered a wooden launder or pipe leading out from the mouth of a bronze age gallery.

Ore concentration

Once mineralised rock was extracted, bronze age miners were faced with the task of removing much of the barren rock matrix around the copper minerals. The object was to prepare an ore concentrate which could then be reduced to metal by smelting. Modern mine operations usually achieve this by exploiting some physical or chemical property of the metal ore through water flotation, chemical precipitation or some such process. While there is no evidence for such advanced treatment in bronze age mines, there is evidence of a multi-stage approach to the concentration of copper ore in these camps. This process began with crushing the rock extract, already very fragmented by extraction by fire-setting, using stone hammers and anvil stones, and then sorting out visibly mineralised fragments to prepare a concentrate (figure 16). While laborious, the efficiency of this approach may be seen in the absence of visible mineralisation in many bronze age mine dumps, most notably on Mount Gabriel, where the concentration of very low-grade ore was a considerable achievement. While water flotation may well have been an option for many copper ores, it is very difficult to obtain archaeological evidence for this form of ore treatment where it was practised in streams.

Many bronze age copper mines are located on complex ore bodies

16. Ore concentration using stone hammers and anvils, Mount Gabriel. (Drawing: Conor Duggan.)

and it is not always easy to identify what mineralised fraction was being targeted. The mineralisation present in these early mine dumps is not always representative of the ore removed during mining. For example, the dumps at Cwmystwyth are full of the lead ore, galena, which was mined there in recent centuries. Bronze age miners at this site were interested, however, in the copper sulphide mineral chalcopyrite, and they appear to have discarded the lead minerals. A particular problem in the study of these early copper mines is to know whether the miners were exploiting primary sulphides like chalcopyrite or the secondary minerals like malachite, which formed as a result of surface oxidation. While many bronze age mines, most notably Mount Gabriel, the Great Orme and Alderley Edge, targeted this surface-enriched oxidised mineralisation, sites like Ross Island and Cwmystwyth confirm that the ability to exploit sulphide ores existed from an early date. What we see in the bronze age is an adaptation to different ore bodies and a willingness to experiment with different types of copper mineral.

Ore treatment at these bronze age copper mines is marked today by the presence of low mounds of crushed rock spoil, often rich in charcoal from fire-setting and marked by a high incidence of broken stone hammers. The equipment used in this work was limited mainly to stone hammers and anvil slabs. A number of bronze age mines in Britain have produced mortars used in ore sorting but these finds are difficult to date, as similar 'bucking stones' were used right up to the nineteenth-century phase of mining at many sites. The discovery of stone mortars and pestles at the Great Orme and of a saddle quern at Cwmystwyth may point to the use of grinding tools as the final stage in ore concentration with suitable rock types. In Ireland there is very little evidence for the grinding of copper ore using this type of equipment, partly because most of the known mines are located on hard siliceous ores. On Mount Gabriel the mineralised rock was first coarsely crushed block-on-block, using stone hammers on the spoil dumps, before being finely broken using the same tools on stone slabs. The use of anvil slabs has also been confirmed in the work camp attached to the Ross Island mine.

Stone cobbles used as rock-crushing hammers were central to the preparation of ore concentrates (figure 17). These rounded cobbles, averaging between 0.5 and 3 kg in weight, with some larger examples in excess of 20 kg, were used either hand-held or hafted to break rock at the mine face and in surface ore concentration. Worn out relatively quickly, these stone 'mauls' are found in large numbers, most notably at Mount Gabriel, where tens of thousands were probably used. Hauling cobbles to this site from local beach sources some 4 km away was a particularly laborious part of the miners' daily work and may even have required special work teams. Many cobbles were modified for hafting before use, to allow either a twisted withy or a rigid stick handle to be attached (figure 18). This took the form of minimal side abrasion in the case of the Mount Gabriel and many of the Welsh examples. Others, such as the Ross Island and Alderley Edge mauls, which presumably lasted longer, were grooved and faceted for hafting (figure 19).

17. Stone hammers from Ross Island, County Kerry, with central rilling to allow a haft to be attached.

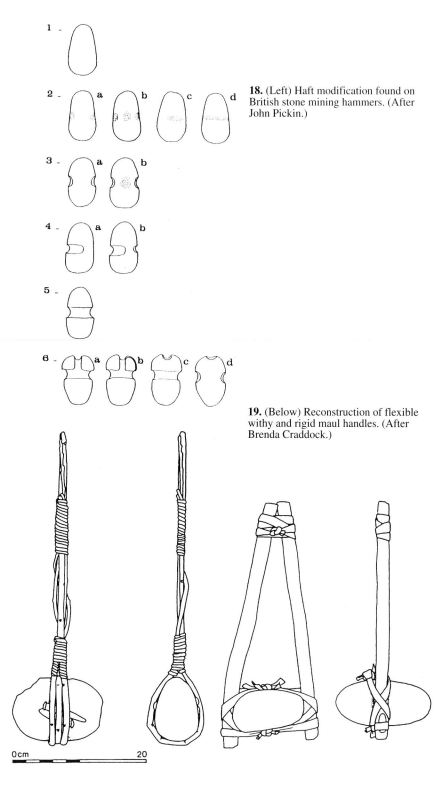

18. (Left) Haft modification found on British stone mining hammers. (After John Pickin.)

19. (Below) Reconstruction of flexible withy and rigid maul handles. (After Brenda Craddock.)

0 cm   20

The smelting problem

So far archaeological evidence for activity in most bronze age copper mines in Britain and Ireland ends with the hand-sorting of copper ore to produce a concentrate for further treatment (figure 21). A particular problem is the almost total lack of evidence for smelting – the reduction of ore to metal at temperatures often in excess of 1100° C in a furnace (figure 20). The absence of slag and furnace remains in these mine sites has been explained in different ways. One suggestion is that early smelting was a very primitive process, possibly at low temperatures, which produced very little slag and so would be difficult to recognise today. Another idea is that this ore was removed some distance from the mines to be smelted, possibly in the settlements from where the mining was organised and where metal workshops may also have made finished objects.

While bronze age copper mining may have been highly organised, it would be a mistake to apply modern principles of management and cost efficiency to our understanding of activities like smelting. So little of the total site area of these bronze age mines has been archaeologically investigated that we should be slow to dismiss the possibility of finding substantial smelting evidence at these locations. This is supported by the many practical advantages of on-site smelting and the discovery of a work camp attached to the Ross Island mines which has produced pit features connected with metallurgy and a few fragments of slag.

20.
Reconstruction of copper smelting. (Drawing : Conor Duggan.)

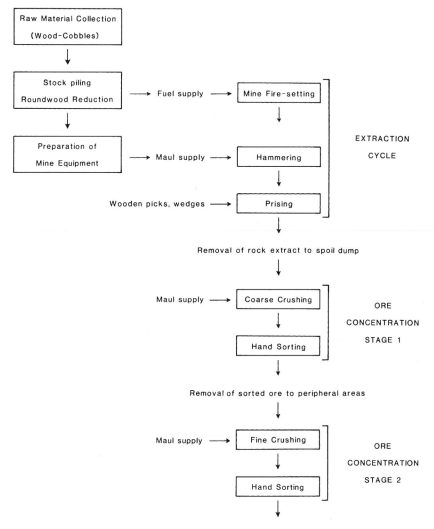

21. The mining process on Mount Gabriel, from prospecting to the preparation of ore concentrates.

5
Bronze age mining in Ireland: Ross Island

The early copper mine at Ross Island on Lough Leane, the largest of the Killarney lakes in County Kerry, has a long history of mining, beginning over four thousand years ago at the end of the stone age. The Welsh monk Nennius, writing around AD 800, probably had this location in mind when he listed the mineral wealth of the lake as one of the wonders of the known world. The mine workings at Ross Island occur in a copper-rich stratum of the Lower Carboniferous associated with calcite veining. This mineralisation was the focus of industrial mining in the early nineteenth century, when some 3200 tons of copper ore were raised for sale to Swansea smelters.

This recent mining at Ross Island uncovered older primitive workings, referred to as 'Danes' mines' in the nineteenth-century literature. Visitors to the site reported 'chambers of rudely vaulted form', worked by 'kindling large fires on the limestone, thereby reducing it to a caustic state'. It was generally assumed that these fire-set workings were destroyed by nineteenth-century operations but recent archaeological investigation has identified important evidence of ancient copper mining. Radiocarbon dates now place the earliest operations between 2400 and 2000 BC, placing the earliest mining on Ross Island in the short-lived copper-using period at the end of the neolithic, which preceded the adoption of bronze.

The bronze age workings at Ross Island survive as large cave-like openings on mineralised exposures in the limestone (figure 22). The mine walls are marked by a smooth concave profile indicative of fire-setting used in combination with stone hammers, which occur in great abundance at the site. These cobble hammers were used, both hafted and hand-held, to pound the fire-weakened face and remove rock. Underground investigation of these bronze age workings is complicated by high water levels and roof collapse, problems early miners may also have had to face.

A large deposit of rock spoil associated with these bronze age mines has been identified. This spoil is rich in charcoal from the mine fires and contains a large number of stone hammers, carefully grooved to take withy handles. Other items of mine equipment include the shoulder-blade bones of cattle used as scoops or shovels to move comminuted rock around the site in baskets of some type. These scapula shovels are

22. Beaker period copper workings on Ross Island.

well-known from neolithic flint mines in Europe; however, the Ross Island examples are the first recorded from an early copper mine.

Of particular importance is the discovery of a work camp associated with the earliest phase of mining at Ross Island, c.2400-2000 BC. This site is adjacent to the bronze age workings and was used for a range of activities including ore concentration, smelting and temporary habitation (figure 23). The foundation traces of several post-built huts, where the

23. Beaker hut foundation, Ross Island mine.

miners sheltered, have also been identified. Food waste, in the form of animal bone fragments, and evidence of hunting, provided by a flint arrowhead and pebble flint working, attest to other activities in the life of this mining camp (figure 24). The animal bones point to an important agricultural base supporting the mine operation, probably located within the immediate Killarney area, where several important metal finds have been made. These include early copper and bronze axes, for which much of the Ross Island metal may have been used. Axes, daggers and other objects made from this metal were probably exchanged widely across Ireland, with some examples reaching Britain.

It is not certain whether the mining at Ross Island was organised on a seasonal basis or involved a long-term commitment by full-time miners. Excavation of the bronze age work camp uncovered spreads of mine limestone finely crushed using stone hammers and anvil slabs. Careful hand-sorting was required to concentrate this copper ore, with the miners possibly using some form of water flotation to separate finer fractions. The ore concentrate was then reduced to metal by smelting in some type of furnace. The discovery of several pit features associated with copper ore and fuel ash sediments suggests that this smelting activity may have been carried out within the work camp area and not removed to some distant settlement. The possibility of identifying on-site

24. Struck pebble flint and a hollow-based arrowhead from the Ross Island mine camp.

metallurgy in further research seasons is an exciting prospect, as no copper smelting furnaces or slag of bronze age date have ever been found in Britain or Ireland.

The copper content of the Ross Island ore body has a varied mineralogy, dominated by sulphides like chalcopyrite and the grey copper ores. The analysis of this mineralisation being undertaken by Robert Ixer of the University of Birmingham is of considerable importance to research into the earliest copper metalwork in Ireland and Britain. Early copper axes, in particular, have long been associated with an arsenical metal of supposed Irish origin. The Ross Island copper ore is rich in arsenic and was almost certainly an important source of this early copper metal. This is strengthened by the discovery of early Beaker pottery, also connected to the earliest Irish-British metallurgy. This pottery has been found in the work camp, firmly associated with mine residues and metallurgical features dating to 2400 to 2000 BC. Some four hundred sherds of early Beaker pottery, representing a minimum of twenty vessels, have been found. These small pottery vessels, decorated with horizontal cord and comb impressions, were used as drinking cups by the miners.

The significance of this find lies in the well-known association of Beaker pottery with early copper-bronze metallurgy in many parts of western Europe. While the interpretation of this pottery and its spread across Europe remains uncertain, many scholars continue to believe in a race of continental migrants who introduced the knowledge of metallurgy to Britain and Ireland. Ross Island is the first copper mine in Europe which can be directly linked to the metalworking activity of these 'Beaker folk'. This site may well become central to our understanding of early copper metallurgy and shed new light on the 'Beaker phenomenon' in Ireland and Britain.

25. General view of Mount Gabriel, west Cork.

6
Mount Gabriel

This mass of Old Red Sandstone rock along the axis of the Mizen peninsula of west Cork was the setting for copper mining during the earlier bronze age (figure 25). Radiocarbon dates for wood and charcoal from these mines suggest that the main period of mining occurred between 1700 and 1500 BC. Some thirty-two primitive workings have been discovered on this mountain, mostly spread out along the eastern slopes to just below the summit (481 metres OD). These small drivings into the hill escaped destruction during nineteenth-century industrial mining in this region largely because of the poor quality of this sedimentary copper ore. The growth of extensive tracts of blanket bog on the mountain has also contributed to the preservation of these mines by masking their surface exposure today.

The earliest written record of these bronze age workings appeared in 1904 but it was not until Duffy's survey of 1929 that the site received wider attention. After much speculation, the age of these mines was finally established in 1966 when another geologist, John Jackson, had a sample of charcoal from one of the mine dumps radiocarbon-dated to

26. Mines 5 and 6 on Mount Gabriel.

the early bronze age. More recently, survey and excavation carried out by the present author has provided a wealth of detail on the operation of these mines and their wider prehistoric context.

The bronze age workings on Mount Gabriel are located on outcrops of bedded sandstone which contain disseminated copper mineralisation (figure 26). These inclined beds are lightly stained green in places by the copper carbonate malachite, which was the main target of the bronze age mining. The mineralised showings were well exposed along the rugged mountain slopes in the bronze age when blanket-bog growth was largely confined to deep basins. The distribution of mine workings suggests a careful and systematic search for these copper beds and an empirical understanding of the geological controls surrounding their exposure.

The mines consist of shallow inclined openings where the copper bed was exposed in a near-vertical scarp face (figure 27). They range up to 10 metres in length, depending on the concentration of copper mineral present and the problems posed by water seepage with increasing depth.

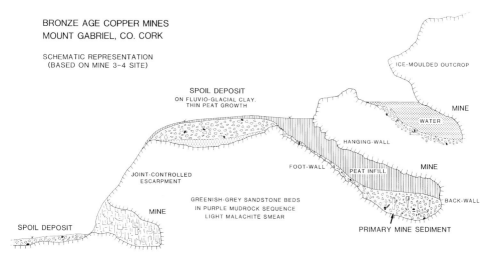

27. Main features of a Mount Gabriel-type mine.

The workings narrow from the entrance inwards, with low confined interiors allowing only a few workers access to the mine face. The two largest workings on Mount Gabriel may reach an inclined depth of 20 metres or possibly more, a considerable achievement in this hard siliceous rock.

The miners worked only in the ore-bearing green sandstones, avoiding the barren purple mudrock, which forms the mass of this mountain. All rock extraction was done with a view to recovering copper mineral, with the miners quickly moving on to other exposures once a particular working was exhausted. The smooth concave profile of the mine walls, together with the high charcoal content of the adjacent spoil dumps, indicates the use of fire-setting in this rock extraction (figure 28). The miners' task was helped where there was a closely spaced cleavage along which rock could be prised out using fingers and wooden sticks. Experiments have shown that up to 5 cm of rock could be removed in this way before the next firing episode became necessary.

Fire-setting experiments have provided a good insight into the use of wood in these mines. Extracting some 4000 tonnes of rock from thirty-two known bronze age workings on this mountain could have consumed between 4000 and 14,000 tonnes of roundwood fuel. A large collection of roundwood branches, many with axe tooling marks, was recovered in a perfect state of preservation in one waterlogged mine. Oak and hazel were the main fuel sources but other species such as alder, ash,

28. Surface fire-working, Mine 3, Mount Gabriel.

birch, pine and willow were also gathered. Wood was also used to make mining equipment, including alder shovels, hazel picks, twisted withies for use as maul handles, oak step planks and resinous pine splints for underground lighting.

Once the mineralised rock extract had been taken out, it was crushed using heavy stone hammers (figure 29) and then carefully hand-sorted to separate out any malachite-stained fragments. The resulting waste accumulated outside the entrance to each mine working to form a low mound of broken rock or spoil, rich in charcoal and hammer fragments.

On present evidence, the mining on Mount Gabriel ended with the preparation of crushed ore concentrates ready for the smelting furnace (figure 20). There is no evidence for this activity on site, nor have any settlement sites with metal workshops been identified in the vicinity. Evidence of metallurgy contemporary with these mines was recovered from a small megalithic tomb some 7 km away, where a decorated bronze axe and two pieces of raw copper were found. The votive nature of this deposit, placed outside the entrance to a sacred site, testifies to the value of metal during the mining period.

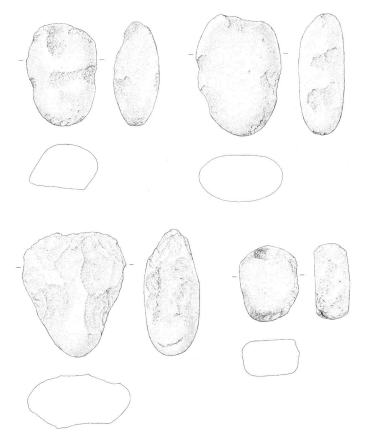

29. Stone mining hammers from Mount Gabriel.

Mining on Mount Gabriel probably came to an end around 1400 BC when the supply of copper-bed ore ran out. The miners moved on to other sources in this region, leaving behind a valuable record of their activity to be preserved beneath developing blanket bog. Mount Gabriel remains the only known bronze age mine in Britain or Ireland to have been spared the destruction caused by industrial mining in recent centuries.

7
Bronze age mining in Wales

Wales has a long and rich mining heritage, best-known for industrial operations of the eighteenth and nineteenth centuries which helped supply the metal needs of the industrial revolution. Mining for copper and other metals at that time led to the discovery of primitive mine workings, often marked by the use of fire-setting and stone hammers. Long dismissed as Roman or medieval, recent fieldwork now places several of these 'old men's workings' in the bronze age – a time when Wales made a major contribution to the development of metallurgy in Britain.

Cwmystwyth

The Ystwyth valley to the east of Aberystwyth was the setting for intensive lead mining in recent centuries, and this led to the discovery of primitive copper workings, now known to be of bronze age date. The early mining is concentrated on Copa Hill, which is part of a complex of lead mines in this area dating from the seventeenth century to the twentieth. A large opencast working and spoil tips containing stone hammers have been identified on an outcrop of the copper-rich Comet Lode, at an altitude of 420 metres OD (figures 30 and 43). This is the only location where copper mineralisation would have been accessible to miners in the bronze age. These early workings and stone hammers attracted attention during the nineteenth century, with the first detailed investigation carried out by Oliver Davies in 1937. Davies trenched three of the spoil tips containing stone hammers, concluding that they were connected with Roman lead mining. The site has more recently been the subject of further survey and excavation, which has shed new light on the early phase of primitive copper mining.

Trenching of the ancient spoil tips in 1986 revealed stone hammers, fire-reddened stone and a few fragments of antler. Radiocarbon dates for charcoal from mine fire-setting have confirmed bronze age mining at this location, c.1700-1400 BC. This rock spoil is mostly derived from a large opencast working, visible today as a depression measuring 45 metres long by 17 metres wide. Excavation has confirmed that this opencast is filled to a depth of at least 7 metres by rock spoil and organic deposits (figure 31). This spoil is rich in lead ore discarded by the bronze age miners, who appear to have been primarily interested in the copper sulphide mineral, chalcopyrite.

Excavation against the north face of this opencast in 1989 revealed

30. Four thousand years of metal mining on Copa Hill, Cwmystwyth. The bronze age workings are located at the top of the mountain (centre), above a network of hushing channels used in mineral exploration in the seventeenth, eighteenth and nineteenth centuries. (Courtesy of Paul Craddock, British Museum.)

31. Reconstruction of bronze age mine operations, Cwmystwyth. (After Simon Timberlake.)

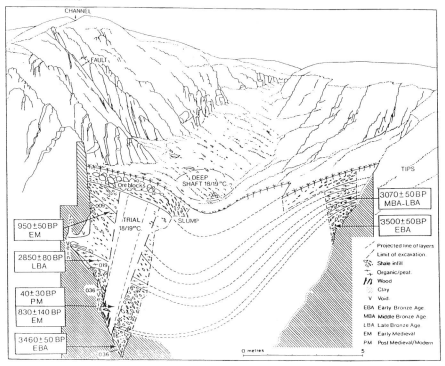

the outline of an arched fire-set gallery extending in at least 2 metres. This mine gallery appears to have been driven from near the base of the opencast, to follow some of the thinner veins running off the main ore shoot. The entrance brow bears the distinctive impact marks created when stone hammers are used to pound a fire-weakened rock surface (figure 32). Several hundred stone hammers have been recovered in investigations at the site. They mostly consist of rounded cobbles derived from a local river, averaging 1 kg in weight, with heavier examples up to 7 kg. The majority bear some trace of hafting, usually in the form of minimal side abrasion or shallow rilling.

32. Entrance to bronze age gallery, Cwmystwyth. (After Simon Timberlake.)

Continuing investigation of the early mine gallery in 1994 uncovered a wooden pipe or launder preserved in waterlogged conditions and believed to have been used for mine drainage. A radiocarbon date suggests that this wooden equipment may have been in use as early as 2000-1900 BC. The working of the primitive gallery and the associated opencast can be linked to lenses of clay containing stone hammers, charcoal and fire-reddened stone. Charcoal from this primary context has been radiocarbon-dated to 1900-1700 BC, with other dates suggesting that mining at this location continued to 1400 BC. The scale of this operation is appreciated when one considers that most of the 3500 cubic metres of rock spoil which fills the opencast today is believed to be bronze age in date. Once mining ended in the bronze age, much of the accumulated rock spoil slumped back into the abandoned workings, preserving them from the eighteenth- and nineteenth-century operations at this location.

Nantyreira

This is another isolated site in the mountains of mid Wales where bronze age copper mining appears to have been carried out. It is located above the 500 metres OD contour on the slopes of Plynlimon. In the mid nineteenth century there was a small mine on this site working a lead-silver lode in Upper Ordovician grits. While the lead-silver may also have been targeted in ancient times, the ore body also contains copper mineralisation in the form of chalcopyrite. The presence of old open-cut workings associated with stone hammers and an iron pick was recorded in 1858. In 1937 the site was investigated by Oliver Davies, who identified an ancient spoil deposit containing stone hammers, charcoal and burnt rock. Davies concluded that the iron pick must be connected to mining in the seventeenth to eighteenth centuries, while the stone hammers were indicative of earlier activity tentatively dated to the Roman or 'Old Celtic' period.

The mine was re-examined in 1988 by the Early Mines Research Group, who identified possible traces of fire-setting on the sides of the old open-cut workings. Trial trenching of the ancient spoil tip revealed stone hammers in association with fire-reddened stone and charcoal. The hammers are mostly unmodified cobbles, though a few bear traces of side abrasion indicative of hafting. Two radiocarbon dates for charcoal place this early phase of mining at Nantyreira in the early bronze age, *c*.1900-1600 BC. Further evidence of ancient mining in the area comes from the copper mine of Nantyricket, some 4 km downstream from Nantyreira. An ancient open-cut working has been identified at this location, where records of spoil containing stone hammers, charcoal and burnt rock are also known.

Parys Mountain

On this mountain (147 metres OD) in the north-east corner of Anglesey there was intensive metal mining in the late eighteenth and nineteenth centuries. An early phase of primitive copper mining, much disturbed by these later operations, has been identified near the summit (figure 33). The focus of this early mining appears to have been quartz-chalcopyrite lodes in the Ordovician shales. Early nineteenth-century records describe the occurrence of stone hammers and fire-set drift workings in this mine. At that time these were thought to be connected with the many finds of Roman copper ingots from Anglesey.

Bronze Age Copper Mining

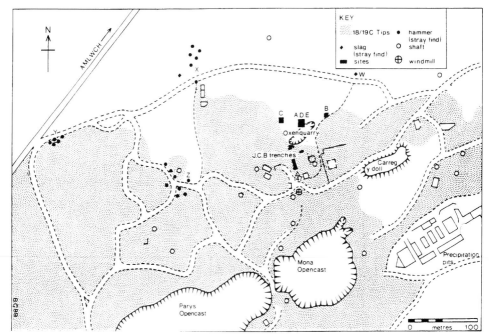

33. Location of early mine remains, Parys Mountain, Anglesey. (After Simon Timberlake.)

In 1937 Oliver Davies trenched an ancient spoil tip containing hammers, which, in the absence of datable artefacts, he also assigned to the Roman or 'Old Celtic' period. This location was reinvestigated by the Early Mines Research Group in 1988 and stone hammers were recovered from an ancient deposit of crushed vein quartz. These cobble hammers are small, averaging only 1 kg in weight, with only a few examples bearing side abrasion indicative of hafting. They can be firmly linked to radiocarbon dates for charcoal from fire-setting, which puts this phase of primitive mining in the early bronze age, *c*.2000-1700 BC. The workings which produced this bronze age spoil tip cannot be identified today and may have been destroyed by nineteenth-century mining. While hard evidence is lacking, a long history of prehistoric copper mining ending with Roman activity is suspected at Parys Mountain.

8
The Great Orme

The Great Orme, a large mass of Carboniferous limestone rising to a height of 207 metres to the west of Llandudno on the North Wales coast, has a long history of metal mining, beginning in bronze age times and continuing with large-scale industrial operations in the nineteenth century. Four major mineral lodes and a series of minor veins cross this area in a north-south direction, with major mine workings located in the Bryniau Poethion and Pyllau valley areas. The mineralisation here is almost unique in Britain, as the limestone rock immediately around these copper-bearing lodes has been strongly dolomitised, leaving it very soft and easily worked using the most primitive of tools (figure 34). The deposits are rich in copper, with the main sulphide mineral, chalcopyrite, exposed at surface and to depths exceeding 200 metres. The bronze age miners were primarily interested in the oxidised portion of this ore body, where the copper carbonate mineral malachite was found in some abundance.

The recognition of ancient copper mines on the Great Orme dates back to the boom period of nineteenth-century mining, most notably to the discovery in 1849 of a large cavern, apparently worked by fire-setting, which contained stone hammers, bone tools and a few bronze objects. This working and others like it were believed to be Roman, a view supported by the investigations of Oliver Davies in 1938-9. Davies excavated a settlement site near the present Gogarth Abbey on the West Shore and uncovered stone hammers in association with Roman pottery. The absence of copper ore or slag, however, cast doubt on this connection and today there is no conclusive evidence of Roman mining on the Orme.

The modern period of investigation at the Orme began in 1976 with underground exploration carried out by Duncan James under Bryniau Poethion. James identified primitive tunnel workings filled with ancient rock debris containing stone hammers and bone tools. Charcoal from this sediment was radiocarbon-dated to 1410-922 BC (HAR-4845), thus providing the first scientific evidence of bronze age mining in Britain. Detailed underground exploration began in 1987-8, led by the Great Orme Exploration Society, which discovered a major complex of bronze age mine tunnels in the Pyllau valley. A programme of surface excavation carried out by Gwynedd Archaeological Trust in 1989 around the Vivian's Shaft area has provided further radiocarbon dates and a detailed insight into the development of this important bronze age mine.

34. Surface workings of bronze age date on the Great Orme. Narrow trench workings are visible leading into a large bronze age opencast, from which there are numerous openings into the underground tunnel system. The modern visitor centre is also seen.

When the Great Orme Mine Company was formed in 1990 a visitor centre was opened which has grown to become one of the major tourist attractions in Wales.

Bronze age copper mining on the Great Orme is of a scale previously unknown in Britain or Ireland. While the true extent of this complex site remains to be assessed, bronze age mine workings have been identified over an area of some 24,000 square metres, with underground passages totalling some 5 km in length and workings to a vertical depth of 70 metres. One estimate has placed total rock extraction in the bronze age in excess of 40,000 cubic metres. This scale of mining is directly related to the soft geology of the dolomitised limestone, which allowed the bronze age miners to tunnel in comparative safety against the hard limestone rock. Not surprisingly, radiocarbon dates reveal a long history of bronze age mining, spanning a one thousand year period from 1700-700 BC as miners moved from surface to deeper underground workings.

Mining in the Pyllau valley began with the discovery of mineralisation along the numerous scarp exposures of bedded limestone rock in this area. A colourful display of oxidised copper minerals on the exposed veins and dolomitised limestone in the Vivian's Shaft area would have provided the obvious focus for initial mining efforts. These began with hand-picking enriched malachite ore from the carbonate host rocks, leading quickly to a series of narrow trench workings to depths of up to 15 metres (figure 2). These trenches constitute worked-out mineral channels from which the ore was removed with great thoroughness using stone hammers and bone picks.

A further stage in this surface extraction was the development of a large opencast to the north of Vivian's Shaft (figure 34). This opencast and the trench workings were taken down to a weakly mineralised level, below which it became necessary to develop a true underground mining system. Surface openings in the opencast area led to a maze of underground tunnels, with evidence of fire-setting and the use of stone hammers and bone tools to depths of 70 metres (figure 35). The shape of these underground tunnels was largely determined by geological controls governing the removal of oxidised copper mineralisation from the dolomitised limestone, softened shales and ore channels. A feature of these workings is the restricted space, with some tunnels measuring as little as 0.30 metre wide by 0.70 metre high. This raises the possibility that children may have been used in underground mining. Many of these underground tunnels, as well as the surface workings, were systematically backfilled with rock waste as the mining progressed.

The discovery of charcoal at depths of up to 70 metres points to fire-setting in this mine, with numerous surface connections providing for

35. Underground mine workings of bronze age date, Great Orme. (After Andy Lewis.)

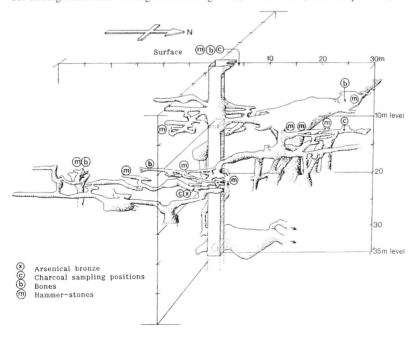

ventilation. The use of this technique appears to have been limited to hard rock, for which stone hammers were also required. About one thousand stone hammers have been found in the surface and underground workings, a small number considering the scale of mining, but reflecting their long use-life and limited application in this geology. These hammer stones are mostly rounded cobbles derived from the glacial drift, ranging from 0.5 to 13 kg, with some boulder examples in excess of 20 kg (figure 36). Few of these hammers were modified for hafting and instead appear to have been used hand-held in the confined underground workings.

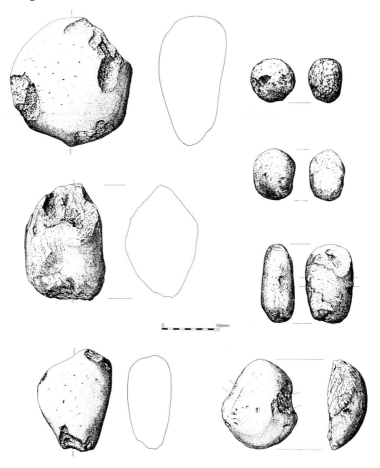

36. Stone hammers from bronze age deposits at the Great Orme. (After Andrew Dutton.)

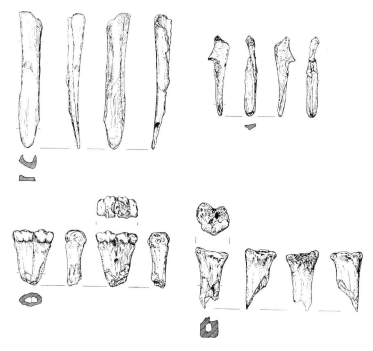

37. Bone picks from the bronze age mines on the Great Orme. (After Andrew Dutton.)

Much of the mining focused on the dolomitised limestone, whose soft rotten texture allowed the effective use of bone and, possibly, antler tools. Some eight thousand animal bone fragments have been discovered in the surface and underground workings, mostly derived from cattle, pig and sheep, with a small amount of antler (figure 37). While some represent food waste, many were trimmed for use as points or picks, designed to scoop out the soft dolomitised limestone. The use of these bone tools in this fashion is confirmed by wallrock traces in the underground mines, which also bear the distinctive impact marks left by pounding hammer stones.

Overall, we are left with the impression of an intensive exploitation of this carbonate ore body over a long period. The miners adapted their primitive technology to extract an enriched ore source in a highly organised fashion, within the controls imposed by the carbonate host rock environment. The scale of operations in evidence at the Great Orme must imply that it was one of the major sources of copper metal in the British bronze age.

9
Bronze age mining in England: Alderley Edge

Alderley Edge is a prominent rock scarp 12 miles (19 km) to the south of Manchester in the north-east part of the Cheshire Basin. Rising to some 120 metres above the surrounding plain, the Edge is formed by bedded sedimentary rocks of Triassic age. Vertical fault movements have uplifted these sandstones, pebbly conglomerates and mudrocks, leaving a block of rocks gently rising from the south and marked by steep cliffs along the northern scarp face. This location attracted human settlement from earliest times, as witnessed by the discovery of stone age flint scatters at several locations along the Edge.

The soft sedimentary rocks which form Alderley Edge are impregnated with copper and other minerals at several horizons. These metallic ores occur as strata-bound mineral disseminations confined to porous sandstones and conglomerates. They are also concentrated along several of the fault zones which cross the Edge and in joint fissures. The mineral ores of copper, lead, cobalt, silver and iron have been found at various times but the earliest mining appears to have focused chiefly on the copper deposits. Malachite is the most abundant copper mineral, coating sand and pebble grains within the coarser sedimentary rocks, where it is also found as thin veinlets. The bronze age miners targeted these soft malachite-rich sedimentary beds, which were prominently exposed at various locations along the Edge.

Alderley Edge and the nearby Mottram St Andrew mine have a long history of mining, the early stages of which have been linked to bronze age and Roman operations, with later industrial mining from the late seventeenth to the early twentieth century. Ancient copper mines were found on Alderley Edge during the large-scale operations carried out from 1855 to 1878. Total ore production in this period is estimated at 168,000 tons, producing some 3200 tons of copper metal, making this one of the richest mines in nineteenth-century Britain. The mining at that time was made possible by the development of an acid leaching process, which allowed the Alderley Edge Mining Company to extract this low-grade sedimentary ore. The working of these deposits uncovered primitive mine pits at various locations, most notably at Brynlow and along the Engine Vein.

The discovery of stone mining hammers and other primitive tools in these 'superficial pits' attracted much antiquarian interest. In 1874

38. The Engine Vein workings at Alderley Edge, Cheshire.

William Boyd Dawkins, Professor of Geology at Manchester University, visited the site and recorded many of the primitive workings and tools then exposed. Further records were made by Dr Sainter in 1878, by which time many of the ancient workings had been greatly disturbed by the industrial operations. A further record of the site was made between 1901 and 1905 by the antiquarians Roeder and Graves, who investigated a number of primitive mine pits along the Engine Vein which they believed were worked with stone hammers (figure 38). By the time mining finally ended in 1919 many of these ancient surface workings and spoil deposits had been destroyed.

For a long time the stone hammer finds remained the strongest indication of ancient mining at Alderley Edge. A large proportion of these mauls were modified for hafting, by using a smaller pecking hammer to abrade or notch the surface or to cut a deep groove around the midriff and butt of the stone (figure 18). This butt grooving is particularly distinctive of the Alderley Edge hammers, many of which are now scattered among museum and private collections in Britain.

The discovery of stone hammers and primitive mine pits, as well as

39. Detail of mine face on the Engine Vein, Alderley Edge.

flints and a bronze palstave axe, clearly points to prehistoric settlement and an early phase of copper mining at Alderley Edge. In the light of recent discoveries in Wales, attention has once again focused on the possibility of bronze age mining here, which was doubted by some commentators in recent years. Hard scientific evidence of early copper mining has remained elusive because the site was so extensively disturbed in recent centuries, as was demonstrated by trial excavations carried out by the University of Bradford in 1991. This research did, however, identify hammer-battered rock surfaces along the surface of the Engine Vein mine which can be linked to an early phase of primitive mining (figure 39).

An important breakthrough was made in 1992 when an oak shovel recovered from the site by Dr Sainter was rediscovered and submitted for radiocarbon dating. The resulting date range of 1888-1677 BC places this find and, through its association with the stone hammers, the primitive copper mining on Alderley Edge, firmly within the bronze age. A Roman coin hoard found in a working on the Engine Vein once again raises the question of copper mining in that period also.

The bronze age copper mining appears to have taken the form of surface pitting on malachite-stained exposures along the line of surface mineralisation, such as the Engine Vein lode. Working to depths of up to 4-5 metres and possibly more, the miners extracted rich pockets of malachite ore by pounding the soft sandstone and conglomeratic beds with stone hammers. Other primitive mining tools such as antler picks and wooden shovels would also have been very effective. However, it is not certain whether fire-setting was ever applied to the extraction of this soft sedimentary rock.

While the evidence is partly circumstantial, our knowledge of the dating of stone hammers from elsewhere in Britain and Ireland, coupled with the radiocarbon-dated shovel find, strongly suggests that mining for copper did take place on Alderley Edge in the bronze age. The site typifies the problems faced by archaeologists when confronted with the disturbance caused to ancient mine archaeology by industrial operations in recent centuries.

10
Copper mining in the bronze age

Many of the bronze age copper mines described above were surface operations in the 0-10 metres depth range. Mining at the Great Orme to depths in excess of 70 metres may well have been exceptional and a function of the peculiarly soft geology and drainage pattern of that mine. It is also clear that the concept of 'ore' as defined today is inappropriate when trying to assess whether a mineral occurrence could have been exploited in prehistory. The search for copper on Mount Gabriel emphasises how bronze age miners were prepared to consider even the poorest of ore exposures.

Work in these mines was undoubtedly hard and, in the case of some underground workings, fraught with danger. While the archaeological record allows us to reconstruct the technology, it gives little insight into the working conditions at sites such as the Great Orme, where children may have been used. Bone waste found in these tunnels may represent food eaten underground, with some workers spending long periods, voluntarily or not, in very confined conditions. As with mining in recent centuries, there may well have been a grim human price to pay for the shiny metal which today adorns our museum cases.

Bronze age metal supply

Scientific analysis of metalwork since the 1960s has provided some insight into the supply of metal in the British-Irish bronze age. The earliest source appears to be a distinctive arsenical metal, believed to originate in south-west Ireland. Production in this earliest copper-using phase was dominated by workshops in Ireland producing simple flat axes, of which some examples ended up in western Britain. Copper-tin alloys (i.e. bronze) were developed in Britain and Ireland shortly before 2000 BC and not long afterwards a new range of metal types appeared in circulation. These new metal compositions reflect the emergence of copper mining and metal production at several different centres in Britain. This pattern was reversed in later bronze age times, when Britain again appears to have relied on imported metal, mostly from continental Europe.

Interestingly, the archaeological record of bronze age copper mining in Britain and Ireland today appears to fit this model remarkably well (figure 40). Ross Island in County Kerry was almost certainly a major source of arsenical copper before 2000 BC. The other radiocarbon-dated copper mines all centre on the early to middle bronze age, with

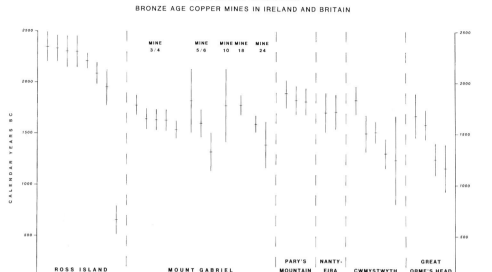

RADIOCARBON CHRONOLOGY
BRONZE AGE COPPER MINES IN IRELAND AND BRITAIN

40. Radiocarbon dates from bronze age copper mines in Britain and Ireland.

most ending operations by 1400 BC. This was also a period when new metal compositions appeared across Ireland and Britain. The only evidence of bronze age copper mining after 1400 BC comes from the Great Orme, and even here operations appear to have ceased by 1000 BC. Access to a major source of continental metal, in the form of ingots, scrap or finished objects, and imported using craft like the Dover boat, may explain why no bronze age mines are known after 1000 BC. Yet this was a period of prolific metal production in both Britain and Ireland and it would be surprising if all insular mining should have ceased. This may well be a problem of archaeological visibility, at a time when bronze picks and other work tools may have replaced more easily broken stone hammers in these mines. Equally significant in terms of site recognition and radiocarbon dating would be any decline in the application of fire-setting.

An industry?

In the past scholars often interpreted bronze age metalworking traditions as in some way analogous to those of modern industries. Major research questions remain to be answered regarding the

41. Stone axe mould from Doonour near Mount Gabriel, County Cork. (Courtesy of the National Museum of Ireland.)

organisation and social context of copper mining in this period. We know so little about the participants in this activity, the way their societies were ordered and the incentives which drove them to copper mining. Are we looking at a type of specialised craft? Were the miners professional, in the sense that this work engaged them on a more or less permanent basis, or was this mining carried out on a broader community level, with everyone helping at certain times of the year? While radiocarbon dating has made great advances in absolute dating, we still know very little about the time-scale or seasonality of different mine operations. This, in turn, affects our understanding of how labour was deployed and the overall scale of production.

Estimates in the past have suggested that the amount of metal produced in these mines may have been far in excess of local needs and, consequently, that it must have been used for trade, sometimes over considerable distances. Recent studies argue that the scale of production may have been much lower than previously believed. In the case of Mount Gabriel, this may have been as little as 15-20 kg of metal per annum over a two hundred year period. This same metal, enough to make forty or fifty bronze axes a year, may have had a wide circulation not as a trade in bulk commodities, but through exchanges involving prestige objects or 'valuables'. A similar scale of production is suggested for sources like Cwmystwyth in Wales. Again, it is interesting that all our radiocarbon-dated copper mines come from the earliest part of the bronze age, when the amount of metal in circulation was comparatively small. One major incentive for these metal producers to engage in some form of metal exchange was the need to acquire tin to make bronze. In the case of the Irish production, this probably involved exchanges with Cornwall, for which there is some evidence as early as 2000 BC.

Many questions, therefore, still remain about the wider production, distribution and consumption of metal. A continuing problem is the scarcity of intermediate metalworking finds – slags, ingots, moulds, unfinished objects, scrap metal – which might shed light on the spatial organisation of this activity on the bronze age landscape (figure 41). Added to this is our poor understanding of the actual demand for metal objects, which have mostly been found in rivers, bogs and other poorly recorded contexts. No major settlement site can yet be linked conclusively to bronze age copper mining in either Britain or Ireland. While some progress has been made, it is proving very difficult to follow the trail of metal which led from these mines. The discovery of a decorated bronze axe and two pieces of raw copper placed as a votive offering outside the entrance to a megalithic tomb near Mount Gabriel provides the kind of information we badly need to assess the role of metal in these societies (figure 42).

What drove these miners in their dedicated,

42. Bronze axe and raw copper fragments from Toormore megalithic tomb near Mount Gabriel. (Courtesy of the National Museum of Ireland.)

0   3
▬▬▬▬▬▬ cm

almost frantic search for metal? Are parallels with stone axe production in the neolithic, with its models of factory-oriented and secondary centre distribution, justified? Can we see the presence of strong individual leaders or 'copper chiefs' whose position derived from control over the production and circulation of metal? This notion fits well with the prominence of individuals in the burial record of early bronze age Britain, for whom metal was an important statement of social position. Such interpretations may reflect our modern capitalist experience and may not be appropriate for societies where the benefits of mining could have spread across a community.

Recent research on early copper mining has shed new light on these and other questions central to our understanding of the bronze age as a whole. This information is helping us move away from a purely artefact focus to the subject of early metallurgy, providing a fieldwork dynamic which in time may address many of the outstanding questions. Important discoveries are confidently predicted within the next decade, when this subject takes a more prominent place in the mainstream of bronze age studies.

43. The search for bronze age copper mines: an opencast mine on Copa Hill, Cwmystwyth, dated to the second millennium BC. (Courtesy of Paul Craddock, British Museum.)

11
Sites and museums to visit

The Great Orme near Llandudno in North Wales is the best example of a bronze age copper mine to visit in Britain (figure 34). The underground workings have been opened to the public and guided tours are available in season. There is an audio-visual presentation and display of artefacts as well.

The Alderley Edge mines near Manchester are also accessible to the public, forming part of a National Trust park today. Many mine workings and spoil dumps are visible in this complex, though, in the absence of site presentation, the visitor may find it difficult to identify features of early mining archaeology.

In Ireland, the Ross Island mine is presented to the public as part of Killarney National Park. A visitor trail with guidebook will be available from 1997 and there are plans for a major exhibition on the mining history and archaeology of this site once the current research project ends.

The public are not encouraged to visit the Mount Gabriel mines because of the fragile blanket-bog environment in which they are located. Anyone visiting this and other bronze age copper mines in Britain and Ireland should remember that these sites are protected by law from interference. Please do not collect artefacts or rock samples. Wear good strong boots and at all times be alert to the dangers of open mine shafts. Always visit old mining sites in the company of others.

Many large museums in Britain have a display of bronze age metal objects and metalworking technology, as does the National Museum of Ireland in Dublin and the Public Museum in Cork city.

12
Further reading

Burgess, Colin. *The Age of Stonehenge*. J. M. Dent, 1980. Background information on bronze age metalwork in Britain.

Crew, Peter and Susan (editors). *Early Mining in the British Isles* (Occasional Paper number 1). Snowdonia National Park Study Centre, 1990. The best collection of articles on bronze age copper mining in Britain.

Holgate, Robin. *Prehistoric Flint Mines* (Shire Archaeology number 67). Shire, 1991. Information on neolithic flint mining.

O'Brien, William. *Mount Gabriel: Bronze Age Mining in Ireland* (Bronze Age Studies number 3). Galway University Press, 1994.

Pearce, Susan M. *Bronze Age Metalwork in Southern Britain* (Shire Archaeology number 39). Shire, 1984. Background information on bronze age metalwork.

Shepherd, R. *Ancient Mining*. C. & H. Publishers, 1993. Background information on early mining.

Tylecote, Ron. *A History of Metallurgy*. Institute of Metals, London, 1992. Background information on early mining.

Waddell, John, and Twohig, Elizabeth Shea (editors). *Ireland in the Bronze Age*. Stationery Office, Dublin, 1995. The proceedings of the 1995 Dublin conference of the same name; contains much that is relevant to bronze age metallurgy in Ireland.

Index